JESSICA NAZARIO

DEVOTIONAL
OF
LIBERATION

For
WOMEN

Devotional of Liberation for Women
Jessica Nazario
© 2024 TX 9-427-138
jnaza2011.jn@gmail.com

Cabo Rojo, Puerto Rico

Dedication

To God, my rock and my savior, who guided me in the darkest moments and showed me the power of His deliverance. To You, Lord, my Liberator and Redeemer, I dedicate this devotional.

Because in my darkest moments, you were my light. In my struggles, you were my strength. Each topic written here is a testimony of Your immense love and transforming power in my life.

Thank you for sustaining me, for liberating me, and for giving me the courage to share my story. May this book be a reflection of Your grace and an instrument to bring hope and deliverance to others.

To You be all the glory, today and always.
Amen.

Gratitude

To Yudi Maleck, with immense gratitude.
I thank God for your life, Yudi, because you were
the voice He used to give me the divine instruction
to write this devotional.

Your faith, courage, and willingness to be used by
God were fundamental for this project to see the
light. Thank you for believing in me and for being a
channel of His grace. Your words were a reminder
of God's faithfulness and His perfect plan.

This devotional is a testimony not only of my
deliverance, but also of the purpose God has for all
those who surrender to His will.
May the Lord continue to bless and guide you
in every step you take.

Thank you very much!

Preface

I want you to know that this book is born from the deep longing of my heart to do God's will, knowing that He longs for every woman through my experiences to walk in the freedom He has promised. We live in a world full of challenges, where many times the chains of the past, emotional wounds, and internal struggles keep us from experiencing the abundant life that Jesus offers us. As women, we face unique pressures that can lead us to feel trapped, hopeless, and far from divine purpose.

Throughout the pages of this devotional, I desire that you find words that speak directly to your soul, that remind you of who you are in Christ, and that offer you the key to open those doors that have remained closed for too long. This is not just a book; it is a journey toward healing, restoration, and true liberation.

My prayer is that each day, as you meditate on the Scriptures and the reflections presented here, you will feel the presence of the Holy Spirit ministering to your heart, renewing your mind, and giving you the strength to break away from all that has held you captive. May this devotional be an instrument in God's hands to guide you toward a full and abundant life, free from bondage and filled with His peace.

Today I want to pray this prayer for each one of you with a heart full of hope and faith, asking for divine intervention in your lives.

Dear God, I ask you to send your Holy Spirit to fill them with your love, peace and strength.
Heavenly Father, break the chains that bind them, whether emotional, spiritual or physical. Heal their wounds, restore their spirit and renew their mind.

Allow them to experience your unconditional love and healing grace so that they can walk in the freedom that only you can give.

Give them the courage to face each day with faith and hope, knowing that in you they find refuge and strength. May this devotional be a powerful tool in their hands, guiding them to a life of fulfillment, peace and purpose in Christ.

I thank you, Lord, for each one of these women. May they feel your presence in every step of their path and may your light always shine in their lives.
In the mighty name of Jesus.

Amen

Introduction

As a woman in life's journey, we all face
challenges that can lead us to feel trapped,
whether due to emotional, spiritual or
physical problems. This devotional of deliverance is born
with the purpose of guiding us toward the freedom and
restoration that only God can offer.

Throughout these pages, you will find
daily reflections, powerful prayers and biblical
passages that will help you renew your mind,
strengthen your faith and experience liberation in every
area of your life. Each devotional is designed to
bring you closer to the presence of God, reminding you
that you are not alone in this struggle and that His power
is greater than any obstacle you face.

My wish is that, through this devotional, you
can discover the peace, hope and strength that God
has for you. May you feel His transforming love
and His hand guiding you toward a full and free life every
day. So, as you embark on this journey of
deliverance, open your heart, allow God to work in you,
and prepare to witness His redeeming power. Welcome
to a journey of faith and freedom!

Physical Release

In our daily walk, the body is the temple
that God has given us to live and serve Him. However,
many times we find ourselves carrying
ailments, illnesses, and physical limitations
that can sap our energy and spirit. In
the midst of these struggles, it is vital to remember
that our God is a God of healing and restoration.

The Bible reminds us in Isaiah 53:5 "that
by His stripes we have been healed."

Jesus, in His earthly ministry, demonstrated again and
again His power to heal and deliver those
who suffered in their body. He has not changed; His
power remains the same today. As we pray for
physical deliverance, let us approach God with faith,
believing that He has the power to heal every
ailment.

May this reflection inspire you to seek physical
deliverance with the certainty that God hears you and
wants the best for you. In His timing and according to
His perfect will, you will experience the healing and
renewal that only He can give.

Prayer:

Dear God, I pray for my physical deliverance. I come to you with faith, believing that you have the power to heal every ailment. I ask that you restore my strength, renew my cells, and give me the health I need to fulfill your purpose in my life. I trust that you are working, even when I do not see immediate results. I thank you for the healing that has already begun in me. In Jesus' name, amen.

let it out

Day 2

Spiritual Release

In the world we live in, it is easy to feel trapped by worries, fears, and spiritual burdens that keep us from the peace and freedom that God desires for us. Spiritual liberation is a divine gift that allows us to break the invisible chains that bind us and prevent us from living fully in the light of Christ.

In John 8:36, Jesus assures us, "So if the Son sets you free, you will be free indeed."

This promise reminds us that our liberation does not depend on our strength, but on the transforming power of Jesus Christ. By giving Him our struggles and allowing Him to work in our lives, we are freed from the oppression, sin, and guilt that weigh us down.

Spiritual liberation begins with an act of faith and humility, recognizing our need for God and allowing His Holy Spirit to work in us. Through prayer, meditation on His Word, and fellowship with other believers, we can experience a profound renewal of our being. This liberation allows us to live with a heart filled with hope, peace, and joy, knowing that we are beloved sons and daughters of a God who has set us free.

Prayer:

Dear God, I want to experience a profound renewal in my being. Allow me to live with a heart full of hope, peace and joy, knowing that I am a beloved daughter of a God who has set me free. Allow Your light to illuminate every corner of my soul, so that I may walk in the freedom that only You can offer me.
In the name of Jesus, amen.

let it out

Day 3

Mental Release

Our mind is a battlefield where many of our daily struggles take place.

Anxieties, fears, worries, and negative thoughts can trap us and rob us of peace. However, God offers us a complete deliverance from these mental burdens.

The Bible exhorts us in Romans 12:2 to "not be conformed to this world, but to be transformed by the renewing of our mind." This implies that true mental deliverance begins when we allow God's Word to renew our thoughts and fill us with His truth.

Jesus invites us to unload our burdens on Him, and this includes our mental burdens. As we give Him our negative thoughts and our worries, He gives us His peace in return, a peace that surpasses all understanding (Philippians 4:7).

We do not have to fight alone; His Holy Spirit guides us and gives us the strength to take every thought captive and submit it to the obedience of Christ (2 Corinthians 10:5).

Prayer:

Dear God, I cast my mental burdens upon You.
I give You my negative thoughts and worries. I ask for
Your help to renew my mind and fill it with thoughts
of hope, love, and faith. Let Your truth be the anchor
of my mind, and may I experience the freedom and
peace You promise me.
In Jesus' name, amen.

let it out

Day 4

Release from the Past

The past can be a weight we carry on our shoulders, full of mistakes, hurts, and regrets. It can keep us from moving forward and enjoying the present, keeping us trapped in cycles of guilt and pain.

However, God offers us complete and true freedom from the past. 2 Corinthians 5:17 says, "Therefore if anyone is in Christ, he is a new creation; old things have passed away; behold, all things have become new." In Christ, we are renewed, our old faults and hurts no longer have power over us.

God calls us to leave behind what no longer serves us and embrace the new life He offers us. This does not mean completely forgetting the past, but learning from it, healing, and moving forward with the confidence that God has a bright future for us.

Through His grace, we can release the chains that bind us to yesterday and walk in the freedom and fullness that He promises us.

Prayer:

Dear God, help me to leave behind what no longer serves me and embrace the new life You offer me. Through Your grace, I can release the chains that bind me to yesterday and walk in the freedom and fulfillment You have promised me.

In Jesus' name, amen.

let it out

Day 5

Release from Fear

Fear is a powerful emotion that can paralyze us, rob us of peace, and limit us in our walk with God. However, the Bible repeatedly reminds us not to fear.

In 2 Timothy 1:7 we are told, "For God has not given us a spirit of fear, but of power and of love and of a sound mind."

Freedom from fear involves trusting fully in God and His perfect love. 1 John 4:18 teaches us that "perfect love casts out fear." When we understand and accept how much God loves us, we can face our fears with the assurance that He is with us and that nothing can separate us from His love. Facing fear requires courage and a firm faith in God's promises.

Let us remember that He is our refuge and strength, an ever-present help in times of trouble (Psalm 46:1). When fears threaten to overwhelm us, we can turn to God in prayer, give Him our worries, and trust that He will give us the peace that surpasses all understanding (Philippians 4:6).

Prayer:

Dear God, help me overcome my fears and trust in Your power and love. Strengthen my heart with courage and faith. I ask that You free me from the fear that paralyzes my life and limits my faith. I trust in Your power and Your love, and I know that You have given me a spirit of courage and self-control. Help me live each day without fear, trusting fully in Your guidance and protection.
In Jesus' name, amen.

let it out

Day 6

Release from Relationships

Relationships are a vital part of our lives, but not all relationships are healthy or uplifting. Sometimes, we find ourselves entangled in relationships that hurt us, drain us emotionally, or take us away from our purpose in God.

The Bible teaches us in 1 Corinthians 15:33, "Do not be deceived: Bad company corrupts good morals."

This verse reminds us of the importance of surrounding ourselves with people who build us up and bring us closer to God, rather than taking us away from Him.

Freeing ourselves from toxic relationships can be a painful and challenging process, but it is necessary for our well-being and spiritual growth.

By taking this step, we are making room for God to connect us with people who will support us, encourage us, and help us grow in our faith.

Prayer:

Dear God, I thank you for your love and guidance in my life. Today I ask that you give me the wisdom and strength to discern and release relationships that are not healthy for me. Help me surround myself with people who draw me closer to you and build me up in my spiritual walk. Give me peace and comfort as I let go of what is not good for me and open new doors for relationships that reflect your love and truth. In Jesus' name, amen.

let it out

Day 7

Release from the Roots of Bitterness

Bitterness is like a deep root that takes hold in our hearts, affecting our peace, relationships, and our relationship with God. When we allow bitterness to take root in our hearts, we move away from God's grace and love. This bitterness can arise from past hurts, unresolved resentments, or injustices we have suffered.

Hebrews 12:15 warns us, "Take heed to yourself that anyone falls short of the grace of God; or else some root of bitterness springing up will hinder you, and through it many may be defiled."

However, God calls us to forgive and let go of these burdens so that we can experience His peace and freedom. The key to freedom from bitterness is to forgive, just as Christ has forgiven us.

Ephesians 4:31-32 exhorts us: "Let all bitterness, wrath, anger, clamor, and slander be put away from you, with all malice. Be kind to one another, tenderhearted, forgiving one another, just as God in Christ forgave you."

Prayer:

Dear God, I ask that you search my heart and show me any roots of bitterness that are affecting my life. Help me to forgive those who have hurt me and to let go of all resentment. Pour out Your love into my heart and heal my wounds. May Your peace and grace fill my life, freeing me from all bitterness. In Jesus' name, amen.

let it out

Day 8

Stress Release

Stress is a burden that many of us carry daily, affecting our mind, body, and spirit. It robs us of peace and joy, and prevents us from fully enjoying the life God has given us. However, God offers us a way to free ourselves from this burden.

In Matthew 11:28, Jesus invites us to find rest in Him: "Come to me, all of you who are weary and burdened, and I will give you rest."

This passage reminds us that we are not alone in our struggles. We can bring our worries and burdens to Jesus, who offers rest and peace. By trusting in Him and learning to live according to His teachings, we find the strength and relief we need to face difficulties with serenity.

When stress overwhelms us, let us remember to go to God in prayer, giving Him our anxieties and trusting in His love and care. In doing so, we allow His peace to reign in our hearts and minds, replacing stress with a deep sense of calm and security.

Prayer:

Dear God, I come before You today burdened with worries and stress. I recognize that I cannot carry these burdens alone. I ask that You take my worries and give me Your peace. Help me to trust in You in every situation, knowing that You are in control. Thank You for Your unconditional love and the promise of rest in You.
In Jesus' name, amen.

let it out

Day 9

Release from Low Self-Esteem

Low self-esteem can be a heavy burden, affecting the way we see ourselves and limiting our potential. However, God calls us to see ourselves as He sees us: valuable, loved, and purposeful.

In Psalm 139:14, the psalmist declares, "I praise you for I am fearfully made; your works are marvelous, and I know this!"

God has created us in His image, and each of us is unique and precious in His sight. When we struggle with low self-esteem, it is important to remember that our identity is not based on our abilities, appearance, or accomplishments, but on who we are in Christ. We are children of God, redeemed by His love and called to live lives filled with purpose and meaning.

To break free from low self-esteem, we must renew our minds with the truth of God's Word. By meditating on verses that affirm our worth in Christ, we can begin to see ourselves the way God sees us. Let us trust that God has a plan for each of us and that He has equipped us with everything we need to fulfill it.

Prayer:

Dear God, thank You for reminding me that I am a
wonderful creation, and that I am of incalculable
value in Your eyes. Help me to see You through Your
love and trust in the purpose You have placed in my
life. Renew my mind with Your truth and
set me free from low self-esteem. Allow me to walk
with confidence knowing that I am loved, valued, and
called to great things in Christ Jesus. Amen.

let it out

Day 10

Release from lack of Identity

In today's world, many women struggle with a
lack of identity, feeling lost or unsure
about who they are and what their purpose is.
However, God's Word gives us clarity and
affirmation about our true identity.

In 1 Peter 2:9, we are reminded, "But you are
a chosen race, a royal priesthood, a holy nation,
God's own possession, that you may declare the
mighty deeds of him who called you out of darkness
into his marvelous light."

Understanding that we are children of God and that
we belong to his family, gives us a solid foundation
for our identity. We are not defined by
our mistakes, failures, or the opinions of others,
but by God's love and truth. He has created us
with a purpose and called us by our name.

To break free from identitylessness,
we need to renew our minds with God's truth,
constantly remembering who we are in Christ. We
must reject the lies the enemy tries to whisper in our
ears and embrace the truth that we are loved,
valuable, and chosen by God.

Prayer:

Dear God, thank you for reminding me that I am your daughter, loved and chosen by you. Help me understand and accept my true identity in Christ. Renew my mind with your truth and free me from any thoughts that make me doubt who I am. May I walk each day with the certainty that I belong to you and that my value is in your love and purpose for my life. In Jesus' name, amen.

let it out

Day 11

Release from Depression

Depression is a silent battle that affects many women, robbing them of joy and hope. However, God's Word offers us comfort and strength in the midst of these dark times.

In Psalm 34:17-18, we find a comforting promise: "The righteous cry out, and the Lord hears them; He delivers them from all their troubles. The Lord is near to the brokenhearted and saves those who are crushed in spirit."

This verse reminds us that God hears our cries and is near us in our most difficult times. We are not alone in our struggle with depression. God is present, ready to sustain us and give us His peace. As we draw near to Him, we can find hope and strength to overcome sadness and discouragement.

It is important to remember that seeking help is an act of courage. Talking to a counselor, pastor, or trusted friend can be a crucial step toward healing. God uses the people around us to offer support and guidance.

Prayer:

Dear God, in this time of darkness, I cry out to You for deliverance. I know that You are near to the brokenhearted and that You hear my cries. I ask that You give me the strength to overcome depression and fill me with Your peace that surpasses all understanding. Help me to feel Your presence and to remember that I am never alone. Surround my life with people who can offer me support and guidance. I trust in Your love and Your power to heal me. In Jesus' name, amen.

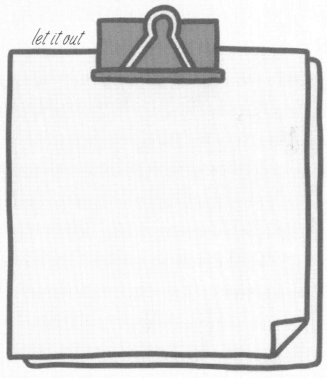

let it out

Day 12

Release from Emotional Attachment

Emotional attachment to people, situations, or things can be a burden that prevents us from moving forward in our spiritual and personal lives. These attachments can create a dependency that keeps us from the freedom that God desires for us. It is important to remember that our security and value should not depend on anything or anyone in this world, but on our relationship with God.

In Matthew 6:33, Jesus tells us: "Seek first the kingdom of God and his righteousness, and all these things will be given to you as well."

This verse reminds us that when we put God first, He takes care of supplying all our needs and freeing us from the emotional bonds that hold us back. To free ourselves from emotional attachment, we must learn to trust God fully, giving Him our anxieties and dependencies.

This involves recognizing that only He can satisfy our deepest needs and give us lasting peace. In doing so, we begin to experience inner freedom that allows us to live according to His will.

Prayer:

Dear God, I come before You acknowledging that I have placed my trust and security in things and people instead of You. Today I ask You to help me break free from these emotional attachments that have bound me. Help me to put my trust fully in You and to seek Your kingdom first. Renew my mind and heart so that I can experience the freedom that only You can give.
In Jesus' name, amen.

let it out

Day 13

Release From Anxiety

Anxiety can be an overwhelming weight that affects our minds and our well-being. It leads us to worry about the future, about what we cannot control, and it keeps us from the peace that God desires for us. However, in the midst of our worries, the Bible offers us a path to deliverance.

In Philippians 4:6-7 we are told, "Do not be anxious about anything, but in every situation, by prayer and petition, and the peace of God, which surpasses all understanding, will guard your hearts and minds in Christ Jesus."

This verse reminds us that we can give our anxieties to God, who will take care of what worries us and give us inexplicable peace. Deliverance from anxiety begins with giving our worries to God in prayer. When we come to Him with an open and sincere heart, we find comfort and security.

He is willing to take our burdens and offer us His peace, which does not depend on circumstances, but on His love and faithfulness.

Prayer:

Dear God, I thank You for Your promise of peace in the midst of anxiety. Today, I place my worries and fears into Your hands. Help me to trust You in every moment of uncertainty. Fill my heart with Your peace that surpasses all understanding and guard my mind in Christ Jesus. Amen.

let it out

Day 14

Release from Sin

Sin, in its various forms, can enslave us and keep us from the peace and fulfillment that God desires for us. We often feel trapped in cycles of repentance and relapse, struggling to find true freedom. However, the Bible assures us that in Christ we find true freedom.

In John 8:36, Jesus tells us, "So if the Son sets you free, you will be free indeed."

This promise is a reminder that freedom from sin does not depend on our strength, but on the transforming power of Christ. His sacrifice on the cross broke the chains of sin and offers us a new life full of hope and freedom.

To experience this freedom, it is crucial to come to God with a repentant heart, ask for forgiveness, and accept His grace. God is faithful and just to forgive us and cleanse us from all unrighteousness (1 John 1:9). By giving Him our struggles and trusting in His power, we can find the liberation we so desire.

Prayer:

Dear God, I recognize that sin has had an impact on my life and my relationship with You. I ask for Your forgiveness for my transgressions, and I pray that You free me from the chains that bind me. Help me to experience the true freedom that only You can offer. Thank You for Your immense grace and for the sacrifice of Jesus that gives me the opportunity to live a new life. I trust in Your power to transform my heart and walk in Your truth. In Jesus' name, amen.

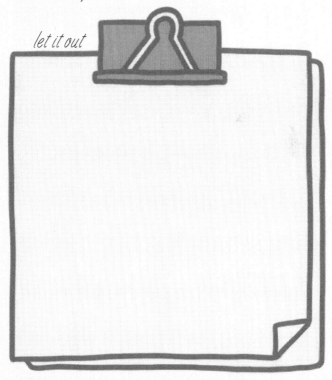

let it out

Day 15

Release from bad Habits

Bad habits can be like chains that bind us and prevent us from living the full life God desires for us. They can manifest in many ways, from destructive behaviors to negative attitudes.

However, God offers us deliverance and the power to overcome any habit that keeps us from His purpose. In Romans 12:2, Scripture instructs us: "Do not be conformed to this world, but be transformed by the renewing of your mind, that you may prove what God's will is--his good, pleasing and perfect will."

This verse reminds us that transformation begins in the mind. When we renew our thoughts and seek God's guidance, we can break the chains of bad habits and embrace a life that glorifies God. Freedom from bad habits is not an instantaneous process, but a journey of growth and dependence on God.

It is important to recognize that we are not alone in this struggle; God gives us His Holy Spirit to help us live in accordance with His will and to have the strength to resist temptations.

Prayer:

Dear God, I recognize that there are habits in my life that do not honor Your name or reflect Your character. I ask You to give me the strength and wisdom to overcome these habits and replace them with practices that glorify You. Help me to renew my mind and walk in Your truth each day. I trust in Your transforming power and Your infinite love to guide me to a life free from bondage. In Jesus' name, amen.

let it out

Day 16

Release from Bonds

In our daily lives, we often find ourselves trapped by bonds that limit us and prevent us from fully living the freedom that God offers us. These bonds can be harmful habits, past hurts, resentments, or anything that keeps us in spiritual and emotional slavery. But the good news is that in Christ we have the power to break those chains.

In John 8:36, Jesus tells us: "So if the Son sets you free, you will be free indeed."

This promise assures us that Jesus has the power to free us from everything that imprisons us. His sacrifice on the cross not only gives us forgiveness, but also freedom from all the bonds that prevent us from living a full life.

To experience this liberation, we need to approach God with a sincere heart and a willingness to leave behind what weighs us down. Through prayer and confession, we can give our bonds to God and ask for His help to break them. He is faithful and powerful to free us from any yoke that weighs us down.

Prayer:

Dear God, I thank You for the freedom You offer me in Christ. Today I come before You with a sincere heart, acknowledging the bonds that have been limiting me. I ask You to set me free from all that holds me captive, whether it be habits, hurts, or resentments. I trust in Your promise that if the Son sets me free, I will be truly free. Give me the strength to let go of what binds me and the courage to live in the freedom You have won for me. In Jesus' name, amen.

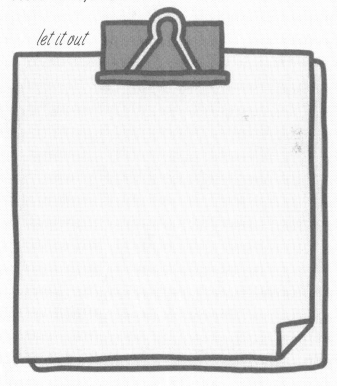

let it out

Day 17

Release from Discouragement

Discouragement can be a heavy weight that clouds our vision and steals our hope. In times of challenge, it's easy to feel discouraged and wonder if things will ever get better. However, the Bible offers us comfort and hope in the midst of our trials.

In Isaiah 40:31, we find an encouraging promise: "But those who wait on the Lord will renew their strength; they will mount up with wings like eagles; they will run and not grow weary; they will walk and not be tired."

This verse reminds us that God is willing to renew our strength when we trust in Him and wait on His perfect timing.

Breaking free from discouragement requires active faith in God's promises and a constant focus on His faithfulness. Sometimes, we need to remind ourselves that even though circumstances are difficult, His love and power have not changed.

Prayer:

Dear God, in the midst of my discouragement, I ask that You renew my strength and give me the hope I need to keep going. Help me to remember Your promises and trust that You are working in my life, even when I don't see it. Give me the patience and faith to wait on You, and the strength to move forward with courage. Thank You for being my refuge and my fortress. In Jesus' name, amen.

let it out

Day 18

Release from Oppression

Oppression can manifest itself in many ways
in our lives: injustice, abuse, adverse circumstances,
or even spiritual oppression. It can
lead us to feel trapped, hopeless, and without
the strength to move forward. However, God's Word
offers us hope and assures us that He is with us to
free us from all oppression.

In Psalm 9:9, we are reminded that "The Lord is
a refuge for the oppressed, a stronghold in times of
trouble."

God is our advocate and protector, always
ready to intervene on our behalf. He hears
our cries and moves with power to bring about
justice and liberation.

When we feel oppressed, it is crucial that we
turn our gaze to God, trusting in His
ability to break the chains that bind us. He
has given us the promise of freedom in Christ Jesus,
who came "to proclaim liberty to the captives and
to set the oppressed free" (Luke 4:18). By putting our
faith in Him, we can experience the true freedom
that only He can give.

Prayer:

Dear God, I thank you that you are my refuge and my strength in times of trouble. I ask that you free me from all oppression that faces my life, whether emotional, physical or spiritual. Break the chains that bind me and give me the strength and courage to walk in the freedom you have promised. Help me to trust in your love and your power to set me free. In Jesus' name,
amen.

let it out

Release from the feeling of Guilt

Guilt can be an overwhelming burden that keeps us from living in freedom and peace.
It constantly reminds us of our mistakes and failures, making us feel unworthy of God's love and grace. However, the truth is that God offers forgiveness and restoration through Jesus Christ.

In 1 John 1:9 we read, "If we confess our sins, He is faithful and just to forgive us our sins, and to cleanse us from all unrighteousness."

This verse assures us that when we bring our guilt to God and sincerely repent, He forgives us and cleanses us completely. We do not need to continue to carry that weight because Jesus has already paid the price for our sins on the cross. Freeing ourselves from guilt requires accepting God's forgiveness and forgiving ourselves.

We must trust in His promise that we are new creatures in Christ (2 Corinthians 5:17), and that the past is behind us. By doing so, we can live with the freedom and joy He desires for us.

Prayer:

Dear God, I thank you for your immense love and for the forgiveness you offer me through Jesus. I confess my mistakes and sins to you, and I ask you to free me from the feeling of guilt that overwhelms me. Help me to accept your forgiveness and to forgive myself. Renew my spirit and allow me to live in the freedom and peace that only you can give. In Jesus' name, amen.

let it out

Day 20

Release from the Anxiety of Failure

The fear of failure is a burden many of us carry, fearing that our efforts will not be enough and that our goals will not be achieved. However, God calls us to trust in Him and His plan for our lives.

Proverbs 3:5-6 reminds us, "Trust in the Lord with all your heart and lean not on your own understanding. In all your ways, acknowledge Him, and He will make your paths straight."

This verse invites us to set aside our fears and put our trust in God, knowing that He guides our steps and leads us toward His perfect purpose. Failure, seen through God's eyes, is not the end, but rather an opportunity to learn, grow, and depend more on His grace and power.

When we face the fear of failure, we must remember that our identity is not based on our accomplishments, but on who we are in Christ. Philippians 4:13 assures us, "I can do all things through Christ, who strengthens me." With this truth in our hearts, we can move forward with courage, knowing that we are not alone and that God gives us the strength to overcome any obstacle.

Prayer:

Dear God, I give You my fears and worries about failure. Help me to trust You with all my heart and to recognize that You direct my steps. Renew my mind with Your truth and give me the courage to move forward, knowing that in You, I have the strength to overcome any challenge. Thank You for Your unconditional love and for always being at my side. In Jesus' name, amen.

let it out

Day 21

Release from the Sense of Inferiority

Feelings of inferiority can be a heavy burden that prevents us from seeing our true worth and purpose in God. This feeling can cloud our vision and make us feel worthless, but the truth is that we were created in the image and likeness of God, with a purpose and incalculable value.

God's Word reminds us in Psalm 139:14:
"I thank you, for I am fearfully made; your work is marvelous, and I know it well."

This verse assures us that we are a wonderful creation, carefully designed by our Creator. God makes no mistakes, and each of us is unique and valuable in His eyes.

To free ourselves from feelings of inferiority, we must renew our minds with God's truth and remember who we are in Christ. In Ephesians 2:10, we are told, "For we are God's handiwork, created in Christ Jesus to do good works, which God prepared in advance for us to do." God has created us for a purpose and has prepared good works for us to do.

Prayer:

Dear God, I thank you that you have created me in a wonderful and wonderful way. Help me to see my worth and purpose through your eyes and not through my insecurities. Free me from feelings of inferiority, and fill my heart with the assurance of your love and acceptance. Renew my mind with your truth and strengthen my faith so that I can walk in the good works you have prepared for me. In Jesus' name, amen.

let it out

Day 22

Release Limiting Thought Patterns

Our thoughts have immense power in how we live and relate to the world. Limiting thought patterns, those that tell us we are not enough, that we cannot achieve our dreams, or that we are destined to fail, can trap us in a spiral of negativity and hopelessness. However, God calls us to renew our minds and break free from these thoughts that keep us from reaching our potential.

In Romans 12:2, God's Word exhorts us: "Do not be conformed to this world, but be transformed by the renewing of your mind,
that you may prove what is that good,
and acceptable, and perfect will of God."

This verse reminds us to allow God to transform our minds, replacing limiting thoughts with His truth and promises.

The renewing of our minds begins by filling our hearts and minds with God's Word. By meditating on His promises and allowing His truth to penetrate deep into our being.

Prayer:

Dear God, I come before You today, acknowledging that I have allowed limiting thoughts to control my life. I ask that You renew my mind and help me see things from Your perspective. Replace thoughts of doubt and fear with Your truth and promises. Help me remember that I am created in Your image and that with Your strength I can overcome any obstacle. Guide my thoughts toward what is true, noble, just, pure, lovely, and praiseworthy. In Jesus' name, amen.

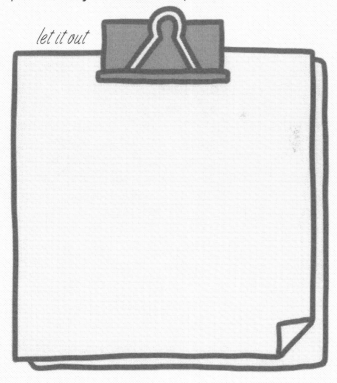

let it out

Release from the Fear of Rejection

Fear of rejection can be a significant obstacle in our lives, affecting our relationships, decisions, and self-esteem. This fear can lead us to avoid situations and opportunities for fear of not being accepted or valued. However, God's Word offers us comfort and strength to overcome this fear.

In Isaiah 41:10, God tells us, "Fear not, for I am with you; be not dismayed, for I am your God. I will strengthen you, yes, I will help you, I will uphold you with My righteous right hand."

This verse reminds us that we are not alone and that God supports and sustains us at every moment, even when we face the fear of rejection. God loves us unconditionally and accepts us as we are. His love for us is perfect and eternal, and is not dependent on the approval of others.

When we understand and accept this love, we can free ourselves from the fear of rejection, knowing that our identity and worth are secure in Him.

Prayer:

Dear God, thank You for Your perfect love and for accepting me just as I am. Help me to remember that my worth and identity are in You and not in the approval of others. Free me from the fear of rejection and give me the confidence to live fully, knowing that You are with me and sustain me. Strengthen my heart and renew my mind with Your truth. In Jesus' name, amen.

let it out

Day 24

Release from Hopelessness

Hopelessness can be an overwhelming burden that robs us of joy and makes us feel lost. In those dark times, it's easy to forget that God is with us and that His light always shines, even in the darkest nights. The Bible offers us comfort and hope in the midst of our toughness.

In Jeremiah 29:11, God reminds us: "For I know the plans I have for you, plans to prosper you and not to harm you, plans to give you a future and a hope."

God has a purpose and a plan for each of us, and His love never leaves us. When we face hopelessness, we must hold on to His promises and remember that our hope is not in circumstances, but in Him.

In Romans15:13, the apostle Paul prays, "May the God of hope fill you with all joy and peace in believing, that you may abound in hope through the power of the Holy Spirit."

Let these words take root in your heart. Trust that God is in control and that He can transform any hopeless situation into an opportunity to grow and strengthen your faith. Even in the most difficult times, His presence is our firm and sure anchor.

Prayer:

Dear God, in the midst of hopelessness, I come to You for comfort and strength. I ask that You fill my heart with Your peace and remind me that Your love and Your promises are unbreakable. Help me to trust in Your plans and keep hope alive in my life. May the power of Your Holy Spirit guide and sustain me each day. In Jesus' name, amen.

let it out

Day 25

Financial Release

Worrying about finances can be an overwhelming burden that robs us of peace and joy. However, God offers us principles and promises in His Word that guide us toward financial freedom.

Philippians 4:19 assures us, "My God will supply all your needs according to His riches in glory by Christ Jesus."

Breaking free from financial bondage begins with trusting that God is our provider. He knows our needs and invites us to seek first His kingdom and His righteousness, assuring us that all these things will be added to us (Matthew 6:33).

The key is to put our faith in God and His ability to provide, not in our own strength or financial circumstances. In addition, God calls us to be good stewards of the resources He has given us.

This involves living wisely, avoiding unnecessary debt, and being generous with what we have. By trusting God and following His principles, we can experience the peace and freedom that comes from knowing that He cares for us and provides for our needs.

Prayer:

Dear God, I thank You that You are my faithful provider. Help me to fully trust You and follow Your principles in my finances. Give me wisdom to manage well the resources You have given me and free me from all financial worry and anxiety. I trust in Your promises and know that You will supply all my needs according to Your riches in glory. In Jesus' name, amen.

let it out

Release from Generational Curses

Throughout history, many families have experienced patterns of behavior and difficulties that seem to be passed down from one generation to the next. These patterns, often referred to as generational curses, can include problems such as addiction, poverty, illness, and family discord. However, as children of God, we have the promise that we can be set free from this bondage through the power of Jesus Christ.

The Bible assures us in Galatians 3:13 that "Christ redeemed us from the curse of the law by becoming a curse for us (for it is written, "Cursed is everyone who hangs on a tree"). "

Through His sacrifice on the cross, Jesus broke every curse that could affect us, allowing us to live in freedom and blessing.

Recognizing the existence of these curses is the first step toward deliverance. When we pray, we must renounce any negative influences that have been passed down through our generations and declare Christ's victory over our lives. It is vital to remember that in Christ we are new creatures (2 Corinthians 5:17) and that His power is sufficient to break any chains that bind us.

Prayer:

Dear God, thank You for Your sacrifice on the cross, which has freed us from every curse. Today, I renounce any generational curse that may be affecting my life and the life of my family. I declare that, in You, I am a new creation and that all old things have passed away. I call upon Your power and Your authority to break all the chains that bind me, and I proclaim freedom and blessing over my life and the lives of my loved ones. Thank You, Lord, that in You we are free. In Jesus' name, amen.

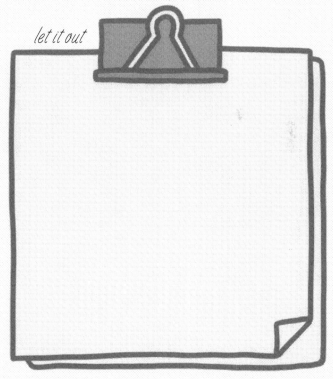

let it out

Day 27

Release from Lack of Self-Love

Lack of self-love can be a heavy burden
that keeps us from seeing ourselves as God sees us:
valuable, lovable, and worthy. Often, our insecurities
and inner critics keep us trapped in a
cycle of self-loathing. However, God's Word
reminds us of our true worth.

In Psalm 139:14, the psalmist declares, "I praise you
for I am fearfully made; I know
what wonderful works you have made!"

This verse invites us to recognize the wonderful work
that we are, created in the image and likeness of God
(Genesis 1:27). When we see ourselves through the
eyes of our Creator, we can begin to break free
of a lack of self-love and embrace our innate worth.

To experience this liberation, we must renew
our minds with God's truth. We must let go of
the lies we have believed and replace them with the
truth that we are unconditionally loved. By doing so,
we can begin to live with confidence and peace,
reflecting God's love in our lives.

Prayer:

Dear Heavenly Father, thank you for reminding me that I am a wonderful creation made in Your image. Help me to see my worth through Your eyes and break free from the lack of self-love that has held me captive. Renew my mind with Your truth and fill me with Your unconditional love. May I love myself as You love me, and live with the confidence and peace that only You can give. In Jesus' name, amen.

let it out

Day 28

Release from Codependency

Codependency is a subtle trap that makes us
overly dependent on others for our
happiness and sense of worth. It leads us to sacrifice
our well-being for the sake of others,
losing our identity in the process. God
calls us to find our identity and purpose in
Him, not in our human relationships.

The Bible reminds us in Galatians 5:1: "Christ
has set us free for freedom. Therefore
stand firm and do not be subject again to a
yoke of slavery."

True freedom is found in Christ, who calls us to live
free from any form of slavery, including
codependency. To free ourselves from
codependency, we must learn to put God at the
center of our lives. This involves trusting in His
unconditional love and allowing Him to heal our
emotional wounds.

As we seek God and allow His love to fill us, we find
the security and courage we need not in people, but
in our relationship with Him.

Prayer:

Dear God, I recognize that at times I have placed my worth and happiness in the hands of others, forgetting that only You can fill my heart completely. Help me break the chains of codependency and find my identity and purpose in You. Give me the wisdom and strength to set healthy boundaries in my relationships and seek Your guidance at all times. May Your love be my source of security and courage. In Jesus' name, amen.

let it out

Release from Nonconformity

Discontent is a subtle trap that robs us of joy and peace. We often find ourselves comparing our lives to others, wanting what we don't have, and feeling dissatisfied with what God has given us. This attitude not only keeps us from gratitude, but it also prevents us from experiencing the fullness of life that God has for us.

In Philippians 4:11-13, the apostle Paul gives us a powerful example of how to live content in any circumstance: "I am not saying this because I am in need, for I have learned to be content in whatever circumstances. I know how to live humbly, and I know how to abound. In all things and in all ways I have been taught to be full and to be hungry, to abound and to suffer need. I can do all things through Christ who strengthens me."

Learning to be content does not mean that we cannot aspire to improve our lives, but that we must do so from a place of gratitude and trust in God. Recognizing and being thankful for what we have, instead of focusing on what we lack, transforms our perspective and frees us from dissatisfaction.

Prayer:

Dear Heavenly Father, thank You for all the blessings You have poured into my life. Help me to recognize and appreciate each one of them. Free me from discontent and teach me to be content in any situation, knowing that You are enough for me. Give me a grateful heart and a renewed mind that fully trusts in Your provision. In Jesus' name, amen.

let it out

Day 30.

Ministerial Release

In our calling to ministry, we often face challenges and obstacles that can make us feel limited or trapped. The pressure of expectations, fear of failure, and personal struggles can affect our ability to serve freely and joyfully. However, God calls us to a life of freedom in our service, trusting fully in His power and provision.

The apostle Paul reminds us in 2 Corinthians 3:17: "For the Lord is the Spirit; and where the Spirit of the Lord is, there is freedom."

This freedom includes our ministry life. God desires for us to serve with a free heart, not burdened by fear or anxiety, but filled with His Spirit, moving with confidence and authority in our calling.

To experience this ministerial liberation, we must surrender ourselves completely to God, allowing Him to heal our wounds, renew our strength, and guide us every step of the way. By trusting in His guidance and relying on His strength, we can free ourselves from the chains that keep us from serving with our whole being.

Prayer:

Dear God, I thank you for the call you have placed on my life to serve you. I ask you to free me from all that prevents me from fulfilling this purpose fully and effectively. Help me to trust in your Holy Spirit, who gives me freedom and strength. Heal my wounds, remove my fears, and renew my strength. May I serve you with joy, confidence, and a free heart, always guided by your love and power. In Jesus' name, amen.

let it out

Emotional Release

Emotions are an integral part of our human existence. Sometimes, however, we find ourselves trapped in negative feelings such as fear, guilt, sadness, or anger. These can paralyze us, preventing us from living fully and enjoying the peace that God desires for us.

Emotional liberation begins with the recognition of these feelings and the willingness to surrender them to God. He invites us to unload our burdens on Him.

Matthew 11:28 says: "Come to me, all you who labor and are laden, and I will give you rest".

In His presence, we find the comfort and healing that our hearts need. Today, I invite you to pause, reflect on your emotions, and present them to God in prayer. Allow His love to fill every corner with your being, and His peace to surpass all understanding. Remember that in Christ, we are new creatures; Old things have passed away, and all things have become new (2 Corinthians 5:17).

Prayer:

Dear God, You did not create me to live in emotional slavery. You have given me the Holy Spirit, to guide me into all truth and help me break the chains that bind me. I open myself to Your love and allow Your peace to reign in my heart so that I may experience true liberation. In Jesus' name, Amen.

let it out

Woman...

You have reached the end of this devotional, and what a beautiful journey it has been! Each page has been a step on your path to freedom, and each prayer, an open door to the transforming power of God in your life.

Remember that this is not the end, but a new beginning. The liberation you have experienced throughout these days is just the beginning of a full and abundant life in Christ. Stay strong in your faith, because God has done great things in you, and He will continue to work in powerful ways.

You are a brave and strong woman. Do not allow doubts or difficulties to make you go back. The same God who accompanied you on this journey is still with you, guiding each of your steps.

Never forget how far you have come and the powerful testimony you carry in your heart!

With all my love and prayers,
Jessica Nazario

Notes

Made in the USA
Middletown, DE
04 November 2024